How to Give Zero F*cks

An illustrated guide

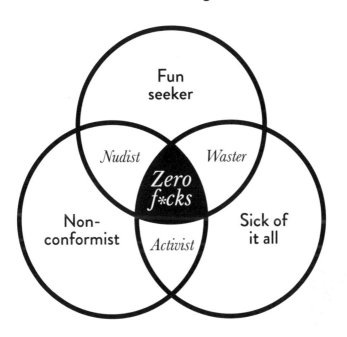

Fun
seeker

Nudist

Waster

Zero
f*cks

Non-
conformist

Activist

Sick of
it all

Stephen Wildish

Blasting off your last fuck
to whence it came

Meh.

Contents

Introduction

Answers to questions like:
"What are fucks? Do I have the fucks?
Can you have too many fucks?"

Introduction

Do you live your life caring what people think of you?
Scared to live how you want?

Learning how to give zero fucks can enrich your life and the lives of those around you. Simply by not giving a fuck you can learn how to be different, how to not care what people think of you and most importantly how to be happy.

```
┌─────────────────────┐
│   Are you happy?    │
└─────────────────────┘
         │
      N ◆   ◆ Y
┌──────────────┐   │
│    Change    │   │
│   something  │   │
└──────────────┘   │
     ┌──────────────────────┐
     │   Congratulations    │
     └──────────────────────┘
```

Do you give too many fucks?

Of course you do, you're on page 15 of a shitty self-help book about giving zero fucks... and you just checked to see if it was the right page number... and now you're disturbed that it's wrong. So yes, like most people you give too many fucks.

People give too many fucks about anything and everything. Unless you're old as shit, old people tend not to give a single fuck. Fucks are flying everywhere leading up to your thirties. You're young and full of hope but life has other plans.

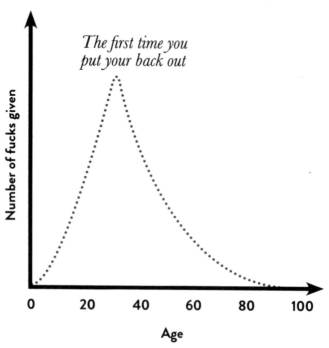

The first time you put your back out

Number of fucks given

Age

0   20   40   60   80   100

Descending to the depths of the Cliff of Fucks to check on stocks of fucks

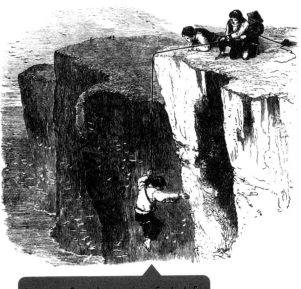

Are you giving too many fucks?

Are you worried about it?

Y | N

You don't give a fuck

Is it important?

Y | N

You're giving too many fucks

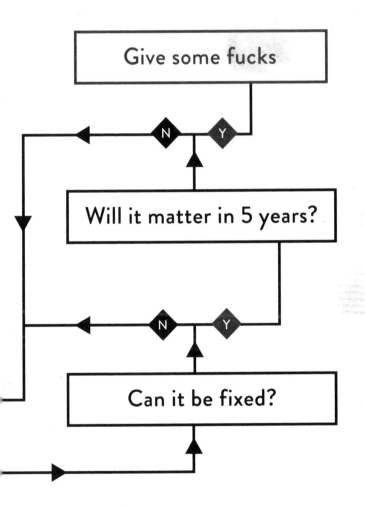

What happens if you give too many fucks

1. You care too much

You care what people think of you,
your life and your piss-poor decisions.

2. You overthink situations

Your mind is a virtual playground for negative thoughts.

3. You get involved with situations that are none of your business

Don't be a nosy nelly. Stay the fuck out of
other people's shit.

4. You think everyone is the same as you

You think everyone cares about your life as much as you do.

5. You give too much

You give out love, feelings and affection like they're going out of date. The cupboard ends up bare and you need to keep some in store for yourself.

6. You're over-emotional

If you find yourself crying at *The Nutty Professor II* or enjoying the film *Love Actually* then you know you've given way too many fucks.

Shoulds, needs and wants

We often give fucks because we feel we "should".
There are no real "shoulds" in life.

There are things you need and want, things you need to do and things you want to do. There is nothing that you 'should' do. "Shoulds" control people unnecessarily. "Shoulds" imply right and wrong.

Do you feel compelled to do something because of a "should"? Take a moment to ask yourself if the "should" is actually true. Can you replace the "should" with "it would be nice to" or "I must"?

The should	The truth
I should feel happy	I would like to feel happy
I should eat less	I need to look at my diet
I should go to the party	I could go to the party
Should we?	Can we?
Should I go to the gym?	Do I need to go to the gym?

Zero fucks personality test

Are you naturally disposed to give zero fucks?
Or are you just destined to care too much?

Have you ever dyed your hair?

a) Yes, loads, and bright colours as well, I'm MAD!

b) Never, people would make fun of me.

c) I do, but to cover up my grey hairs.

What do you drive?

a) A fixie with an airhorn, LOL.

b) A mid-range car.

c) I use public transport.

Do you exercise?

a) Crossfit, OBVS.

b) I like to jog at night.

c) Is drinking wine exercise?

Do you ever call in sick to work when you are not sick?

a) At my tech start-up we are allowed to take 3 duvet days, it's wicked.

b) I only call in sick if I am sick, obviously. I don't want to get disciplined.

c) Not often, but sometimes things are too much to take.

When do you go to bed?

a) When the party has finished.

b) 10pm, I need to be at work 20 minutes early to make everyone tea.

c) I watch Netflix boxsets until 2am.

Do you have tattoos?

a) I'm dripping in them, my arm is an etch-a-sketch.

b) My skin is sacred ground.

c) One small one, but it's a secret that I can't tell anyone.

Can you stick to a budget?

a) My bank account is a designated UN disaster zone.

b) I have ISAs and going over my monthly spending limit makes me feel sick.

c) I use my overdraft regularly.

How did you do? Tot up your scores and see your accurate personality revealed to you below in our scientific test:

Mostly As

You filled out a questionnaire in a shitty book. You're trying too hard and giving too many fucks. Calm down.

Mostly Bs

You filled out a questionnaire in a shitty book. You give too many fucks what people think of you.

Mostly Cs

You filled out a questionnaire in a shitty book. You give too many fucks and need to care for yourself more.

Mostly Ds

You give zero fucks. Congratulations.

What are fucks then?

Fucks are a currency. You have a certain amount of fucks to give and these can be converted to either 'shits' or 'cares'. Moaning that you don't give a shit is not even close to not giving a fuck.

There are more shits to a fuck and even more cares in a shit. Look after the cares and the fucks look after themselves.

I'M NOT BOTHERED

I DON'T CARE

I DON'T GIVE A SHIT

I DON'T GIVE A FUCK

I DON'T GIVE A FLYING FUCK

I GIVE ZERO FUCKS

$$\frac{1}{fuck} = \frac{5}{shits} = \frac{50}{cares}$$

Responding to thirsty direct messages in the 1800s

I DON'T GIVE A SINGLE SHIT

ABOUT YOUR ZERO FUCKS

Absolute zero fucks

Giving zero fucks is a baseline to work from. There is a deeper, darker place than zero fucks given: absolute zero. Absolute zero fucks has life-altering consequences.

Turning up nude to work and fighting strangers on the commute is a signifier that you've hit rock bottom, absolute zero fucks.

**So tired of everyone's bullshit you
finally reach absolute zero fucks**

The fuck thermostat

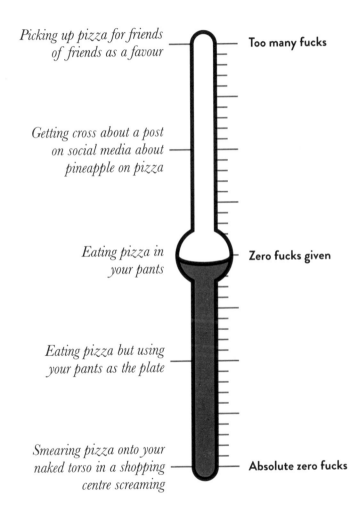

Picking up pizza for friends of friends as a favour — **Too many fucks**

Getting cross about a post on social media about pineapple on pizza

Eating pizza in your pants — **Zero fucks given**

Eating pizza but using your pants as the plate

Smearing pizza onto your naked torso in a shopping centre screaming — **Absolute zero fucks**

What to give a fuck about?

So we have learned that even if you are giving zero fucks, really there are still things to give fucks about (or we would all end up nude with machine guns and that is not a world we should be living in).

What are the things to give a fuck about? Most of what we actually do in our waking hours is completely pointless shit. The secret is to work out which of all the activities you do in a day you can strip away and still function as a human. For example, ironing underpants is a completely useless waste of time and effort.

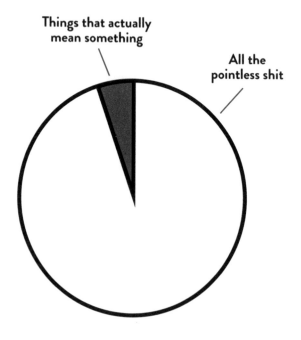

Things that actually mean something

All the pointless shit

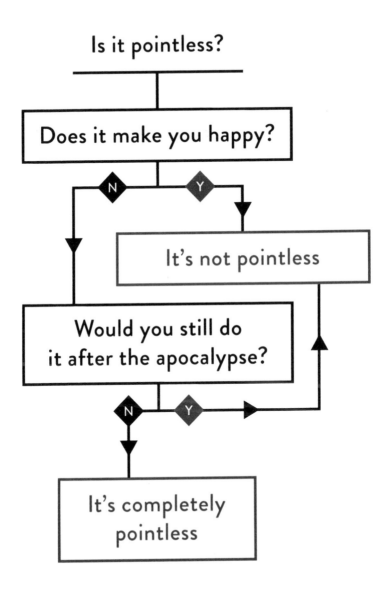

HAVE MORE FUN

GIVE FEWER FUCKS

What's the fucking point?

There isn't one, probably.

You just sent the boss an email with a kiss at the bottom? You want to set fire to your desk and immediately leave the company? Take a moment to think about the vast infinity of space and the unimaginable amount of stars in the universe. Our little blue dot of a planet is pretty insignificant and you in the middle of 7 billion other souls are even more inconsequential.

When you're halfway through counting all the stars and realise it's pointless

"A person is nothing else but what they make of themselves."

Jean-Paul Sartre

"Barbecues every day"

Dr. Dre

Life is finite

Humans spend nearly every waking hour blocking out and distracting ourselves from our own mortality.

The problem being that if we don't recognise that life is finite we think there is always tomorrow to achieve a goal or dream. If you were to recognise that you are running out of time you would surely do more than stare at your fucking phone all day.

So be good, do good things, work hard to achieve something and try to enjoy yourself on the way.

The eternity of time before you were born

Your little turn to be alive

The eternity of time after you die

When you finally complete your goals and dreams
but you're dead anyway so it doesn't matter

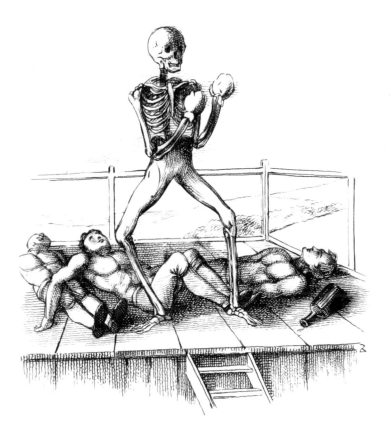

YOU WERE BORN

YOU WILL DIE

(something to write in birthday cards)

At work

Answers to questions like:
"What is the minimum fucks you
can give without being fired?"
and "Can I poo at work?"

At work

Keeping a supply of fucks to give at work is healthy
and to be recommended (this is to avoid being fired).
There are areas to spend fucks and certainly areas where too
many fucks are currently given. Meetings. It's the endless
pointless meetings. They can fuck off.

**Giving a cheeky wink and heading off to work
knowing you will give precisely zero fucks today**

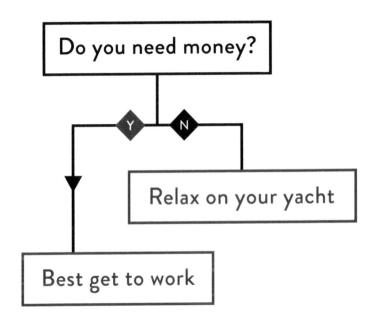

Imposter syndrome

If you're giving a fuck at work because you're feeling inadequate, it's helpful to know that there is a name for this: imposter syndrome. You wonder how you got where you are, feel like you're just making it up as you go along and surely you will be discovered at any minute?

Well, the surprise is that most people have felt this at some point. The key to not giving a fuck is realising that everyone is making it up as they go as well. Nobody knows what the fuck they are doing in reality.

What you know

What you think every fucker knows

Knowing fuck all

But what if you actually know fuck all?
Some people are complete fucking idiots after all.

Ignorance is bliss.

The stages of knowledge

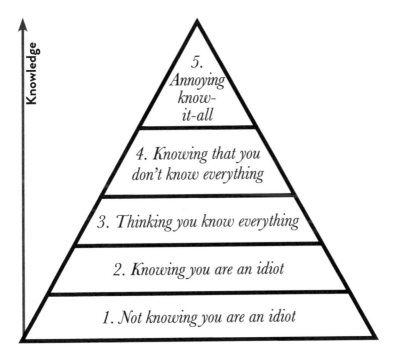

"THE MORE YOU **KNOW**, THE MORE YOU…

"... KNOW WHAT YOU DON'T KNOW"

Richard Feynman

Staying late

At 5pm in offices across the land there is a Mexican standoff happening as people wait for the first person to crack and leave. The participants don't want to be different and to stand out from the crowd. The instigators are simply people making a show of how important and dedicated they think they are. In reality, nobody cares what they think of themselves.

Well, be the person to be different. Arrive at work on time, leave on time. Do the work, fuck off.

As long as you are getting your work done in the hours provided, you are performing well. Anything else is just thirsty for bosses, attention, or worse, poor time management. Probably just stop looking at Facebook all fucking day.

I love staying late at work every damn day.

Not one person, ever

Typical workday breakdown

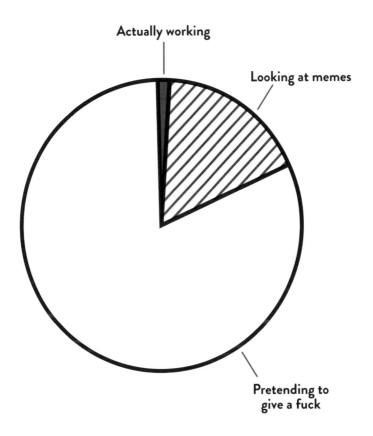

Actually working

Looking at memes

**Pretending to
give a fuck**

Commuting

The process of getting to and from work is fraught with
fucks to give: slow people walking along narrow streets,
late buses and general road rage.

Before you become filled with anger, remember that
these are all people in their own right. Like you, they
have lives, families, futures and dreams. Apart
from people who listen to music too loudly through
headphones. There isn't a circle of hell deep enough
for those pricks.

Should you apply make-up on public transport?

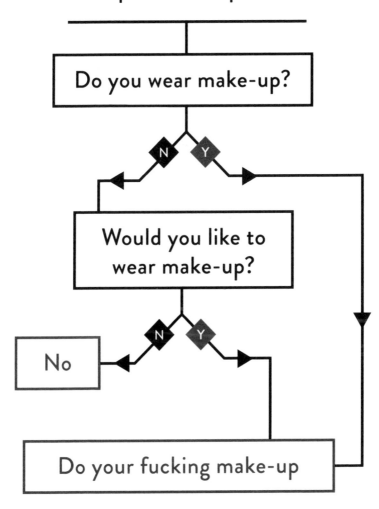

Do you wear make-up?

Would you like to wear make-up?

No

Do your fucking make-up

"PATIENCE IS THE COMPANION OF WISDOM"

Saint Augustine

"PICK A LANE YOU FUCKING DICKHEAD"

Also Saint Augustine, late for mass

Bosses

Bosses can fire you. It's a really good idea to give fucks around them. Only a light sheen of fucks is all that is needed to maintain the illusion that you are actually a hard-working member of the team.

Do	Don't
Socialise with them. But only if they are nice	Let bosses win at sports. That's just brown-nosing
Show interest in their lives	Be friends on Facebook
Make sure your achievements are noticed	Award yourself trophies
Offer to make tea/coffee	Spit in it, you animal
Give fucks around them	Fuck them
All of your work	Blame others if you fail

Don't say

"I don't give a fuck, Karen."

Do say

"Thank you, Karen, I will give this the attention it deserves."

Conference calls

If you can make an excuse to avoid a conference call do it
as they are a pointless waste of everybody's time.

You can easily catch up with someone who was in the
call later and, in most cases, realise that absolutely nothing
was decided so you had a lucky escape. You can use the time
to catch up on work that actually needs doing.

Conference call timeline

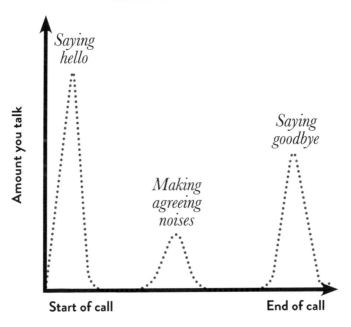

*Saying
hello*

*Saying
goodbye*

*Making
agreeing
noises*

Amount you talk

Start of call · End of call

Lunch breaks

Always, always take your lunch break. The break is there
for a reason. It allows your mind to rest and refocus.

There are those who don't take their full lunch break,
opting to nip out for a sandwich and rush back to
their desk apologising profusely for being so long and
exclaiming that it was "crazy out there" to a room full of
people who couldn't give a shit or didn't even notice they
were gone. A demonstration of someone giving far too
many fucks if ever there was one.

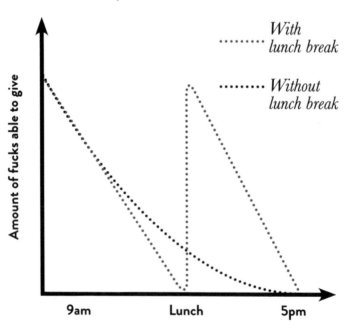

Leave your desk

If you sit at your desk you will either
be tempted into watching cat videos
or Karen will come and ask for a
"quick favour". What a fucking bitch.

Eat leisurely

Take your time, digest properly,
enjoy a walk around a park.

Return in time

Don't take the piss, do come back to work
after your lunch break is over.

Colleagues and clients

You spend most of your waking day at work. You can choose your friends but not your colleagues, so the chances are that at least one of your colleagues will be a complete arsehole.

If office social activities or cultures are not something you want to get involved in, then don't. Don't be afraid to stand out and don't feel forced to do things you don't want to.

Then there are the clients. Dealing with clients often means wearing a shit-eating grin whilst quietly dying inside. They hold the balance of power. The customer isn't always right but pretending they are can spend a lot of fucks!

The client logic gate

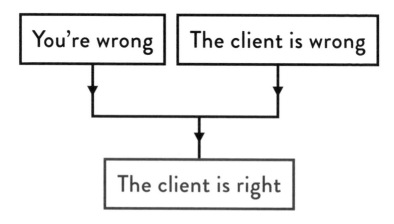

Would you give a fuck?

Your colleagues are having a "bake off"
competition for charity. Do you:

A

Spend the week baking
until you perfect your
12-tier génoise.

B

Turn up,
eat cake,
fuck off.

C

Cake is full of carbs and
refined sugar. No way
would you partake.

You gave way
too many fucks

A

You gave
zero fucks

B

You gave
some fucks

C

DREAMS
+
WORK
=
SUCCESS

WORK

+

ARSEHOLES

=

STRESS

Passive aggressive emails

If you are struggling to give a fuck whilst emailing you can easily disguise your true feelings in some of these helpful phrases:

What you say	What it means
"As per my last email"	"Can you read, dickhead?"
"Sorry to bother you again."	"I am not sorry, you need to do better."
"Great!"	"Fine"
"Great."	"Fuck you"
"Let me know if you need any assistance with this."	"Do not, under any circumstances, ask for my assistance."
"Kind regards"	"Go fuck yourself"
"Reattaching it here just in case…"	"You definitely have this already but you're a lazy, incompetent shit."

The pointless email loop

Thanks

↗   ↘

OK, great   *No problem*

↖   ↙

Great,
see you soon

Not all emails need a reply.

Toilet etiquette

Sometimes you need to do a poo at work. In fact, if you are eating enough fibre you will probably need to go at least once a day.

Holding in a poo isn't always possible and is actually bad for you and bad for your stress levels.

Sploshing and trumps

If you venture into the loo and there are numerous occupants, don't fear a loud splosh as you achieve "touchdown", and if a sneaky fart pops out, own it.

The likelihood is that nobody knows who made the noise and most people will be secretly laughing anyway. If it still bothers you, listen to some music. What better way to drown out sploshes than with a classical soundtrack?

The ungodly smell

Yeah, you can't do anything about that. This is one of those 'smile and overlook it' type of things. Everybody poos. It's one of the signs of life. If you're not pooing, you're dead.

Nobody cares

Do you keep track of the time other people spend in the toilet?*
No, of course not, and nobody is doing the same to you.
Not one person is bothered if you are going for a shit and nobody is timing how long you take.

*If you do you're simply a dick. Stop it immediately.

Have you done a smelly poo at work?

Is anyone in the loo?

Y / N

Can you be bawdy?

Y / N

Ignore it and carry on

"I'd give that a minute."

Making it to Friday

Getting through the week at work can feel like an
achievement worthy of a medal or trophy. You coped.

Not one person was killed at work for being a prick. Go
you. Just as the amount of fucks you have to give finally
reaches zero the weekend hits you. Two days to recharge
and prepare for Monday.

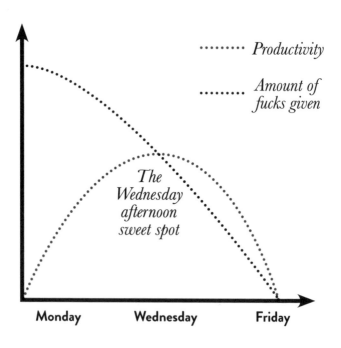

**Leaving after your shift knowing full well that
your workplace is in complete chaos**

"IT HAS BEEN A LONG WEEK"

You in the middle of Monday

"YAY, IT'S FUCKING FUCK OFF FRIDAY"

You at the end of the week

Relationships

Answers to questions like:

"Relationships are effort, should I give a fuck?"

Relationships

You can fall in love with anyone or anything you like if you want to.
Some people fall in love with bridges for fuck's sake.

Making a healthy relationship that works is a different matter
entirely. If you've found someone who will tolerate your utter
bullshit then you're exceptionally lucky.

I'm in a relationship with wine.

Do you want to be in a relationship?

Y — Do you have someone in mind?

N — Great

Do you have someone in mind?

Y — Do they like you?

N — Go looking

Do they like you?

Y — Ask them on a date

N — Go looking

Dates

Dates, and especially first dates, are high-stress situations fraught with fuck giving. You're trying hard to give a good impression of yourself and hide the mess you are inside.

The most important thing to do on a date is listen.
You can then tell if they are an arsehole straightaway rather than finding out months from now.

Don't worry about the outcome.
This applies before and after the date. If less emphasis is placed on how well the date is going to go, you're going to be far more relaxed.

Don't	Do
Order a salad to look healthy	Order what you like to eat
Follow them on social media immediately after the date	Call or text them
Start planning the wedding	Talk about things that are important to you
Talk about your ex	Talk about your future plans
Seriously, don't talk about your ex	If it goes badly, notch it up to experience and move on

How you come across to new people

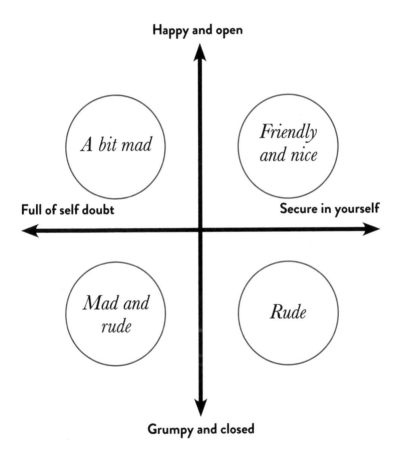

"NO MATTER WHAT, ALWAYS BE YOURSELF"

Dickheads on the internet

" ... UNLESS YOU'RE A COMPLETE COMPLETE ARSEHOLE"

The truth

Valentine's

If you're single, Valentine's day can be a hard time to get through, especially if your perception is that everyone is getting Valentine's day cards except for you. If you think you won't be receiving a card this year then treat yourself gently, maybe give a few cards yourself and use the time to contact a few other single friends.

If you are in a relationship simple statements of love are the zero fucks way to approach Valentine's day. A single rose says so much more than a room full of teddy bears and heart-shaped balloons.

Would you give a fuck?

It's Valentines day and you've received
the sum total of zero Valentine's day cards. Do you:

A

Get a makeover and
start a programme of
self-improvement

B

Cry yourself to sleep and
mope around the house
comfort eating

C

Buy yourself a gift, get a
takeaway and have some
alone time

You gave
some fucks

You gave way
too many fucks

You gave
zero fucks

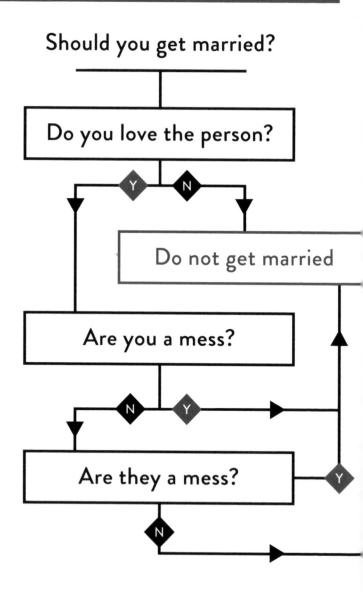

Should you get married?

Do you love the person?

Y   N

Do not get married

Are you a mess?

N   Y

Are they a mess?

Y

N

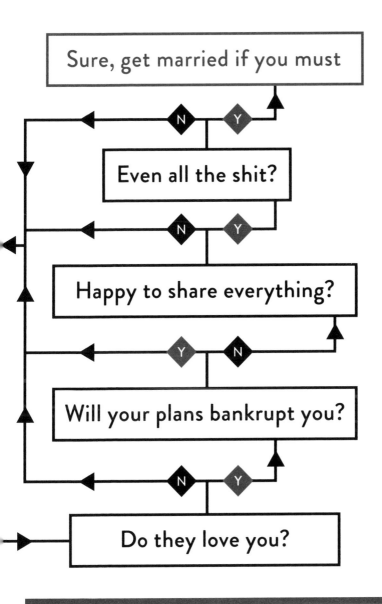

Being single

Society is geared towards people being coupled off into relationships. For whatever reason, it can be hard to be single as you stand out and are different. Stick a single finger up to society and enjoy the many perks of being single.

Whilst single you can work on getting yourself sorted and secure without some prick being needy around you.

Why being single is good

You're a secure and well-balanced person

You don't have to share puddings

You preaching about being single, knowing full well
you're not going outside anytime soon

Relationship status

TABLE FOR ONE

DRINKS
FOR
TWO

Heart break

A broken heart is hard to fix, but with a zero fucks attitude you can certainly help the process (along with a fuckload of alcohol and chocolate).

Instead of focusing on the broken relationship behind you, begin to imagine a new exciting future for yourself without this person. Seek out your more stable friends to console you and make a plan.

For fuck's sake stop contacting them. If they are still in contact with you or sending mixed messages about still wanting to be friends then you need to create some distance. If they wait months and then send you a "miss you" text then that's proof if you needed it that they are in fact an arsehole.

I am	Looking for
⭕ *A man*	⭕ *A man*
⭕ *A woman*	⭕ *A woman*
⦿ *A fat fuck*	⦿ *A discount code for pizza*

Your dating profile

Would you give a fuck?

You get dumped. By text. Would you...

A

Go to their house and cause hell.

B

Go to bed, for years.

C

Reply "New phone who dis?"

You gave way too many fucks

You gave absolute zero fucks

You gave zero fucks

Going out

"Fuck it, I'm doing karaoke."

Going out

Mixing with the general public generally requires far too many fucks. If you do venture out to see friends then prepare to spend some fucks, But spend them wisely.

Small talk

Small talk is the epitome of giving too many fucks.
Overly polite conversation with no real meaning. You can't
avoid small talk but there are ways you can give zero fucks
and come through to the other side smiling:

Ask a decent/unusual question
Don't ask dull questions, they get dull answers. Ask them what
their favourite biscuit is, or if they put milk first in tea.

Listen
If talk is progressing from small to large, listen to the answers.
You might just enjoy this conversation after all.

Be honest
If someone is talking about something you disagree with or dislike,
be honest. You don't have to be confrontational but knowing
you stand on differing sides of an issue can make a good
conversation in itself.

Fuck it
Alternatively, just give people one word answers,
close that shit down and learn to enjoy sweet,
sweet awkward silences.

Hey, how are you?

↓

Doing well, you?

↓

Great, you?

↓

Er...

This fucking ridiculous shit

"GOING OUT IS THE NEW STAYING IN"

Extrovert

"STAYING IN IS THE NEW GOING OUT"

Introvert

Singing in public

For some people the thought of singing in public is enough to turn their arse inside out with cringe. But to others it's something they would love to do. Singing is therapeutic and doing it in front of people can be exhilarating.

Join a choir

Communal singing has been proven to reduce stress and significantly reduce the amount of fucks you have to give on a daily basis purely through the pleasure it brings. If you can't sing, your tuneless warblings will be drowned out by people around you who can.

When you love singing but also your head is a fucking onion

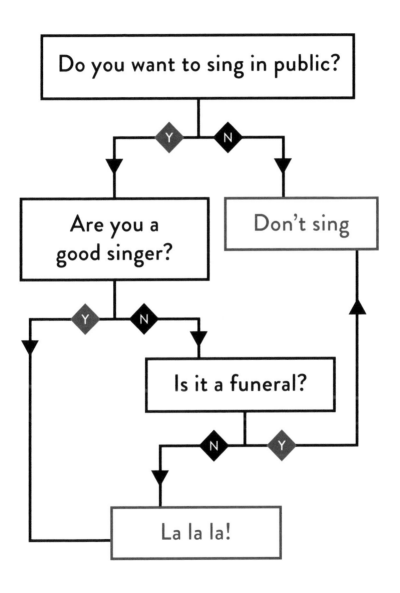

Dancing

If you've watched children dance at a wedding then you know that it doesn't have to look good for you to enjoy yourself. They dance without all the bullshit embarrassments we put on ourselves as adults. Kids are having the best fun dancing.

If you suffer from dance anxiety and want to dance, you can start by dancing on your own. Get the tunes pumping and start a kitchen disco. With no judgements or social stigma you can begin to dance freely. The next step is to take that shit to the dance floor. Don't take yourself too seriously, this isn't *Flashdance*. Have a boogie and feel the music, and be prepared to laugh at yourself.

If you've run out of moves or find yourself shuffling awkwardly, then it's time to bust out the bum wiggle, where you write your name in the air using your bum. Get others around to join in.

Live Love Laugh

Karen's living room wall

Dance like nobody's watching

Karen's kitchen wall

When you realise you have to move house and country and continue your life under a new name

Eating out

Some waiters in high-end restaurants can make you feel like you're not worthy of their fine establishment. This may actually be your own issues of not feeling posh enough to even be there in the first place. Remember that your money is going in their till.

Don't be rushed

Take your time choosing what you want to eat. It's going in your mouth after all. If a waiter tries to rush you just ask for five minutes.

Ask questions

If you don't know what something on the menu is, ask. You might feel foolish but you might learn something. Then again it might just be a posh word for chips.

The wine list

Don't feel pressure to order the second cheapest bottle of wine. If you want it, order the cheapest. Wine is all smoke and mirrors after all.

Don't be scared to get their attention

The end of a meal can be marred by lack of attention from a waiter. You can be left hanging around waiting to pay a bill. Enjoy making the international hand gesture for "Can I get the bill", alternatively just raise a hand to get their attention. It might feel rude but fuck it, it's not like you've given them the finger. Do not give them the finger.

Weddings

At its heart, a wedding is a beautiful day when two people stand in front of their peers and profess their love for each other, and then everybody gets pissed.

There is a lot of pressure for weddings to run smoothly and to be "the perfect day". It can transform perfectly ordinary women and men into "bridezillas" and "groomzillas".

Chill the fuck out

If it's your wedding, accept that some things will go wrong. It's an important day and you will have planned for months so it's natural to feel anxious. Communicate your anxiety to those around you and keep a light-hearted attitude so you can see the funny side of the things that do go wrong.

Don't get too pissed

Enjoy the free booze, but don't get too pissed or you will have a world of fucks to deal with in the morning.

Don't feel like you have to do the traditions

Weddings are littered with many pointless traditions and hang-ups from hundreds of years of oddness. If you don't want to cut a cake, don't. If you don't want to unbutton your bottom button of a waistcoat, don't. As long as there is a ceremony of sorts and booze everyone should be happy.

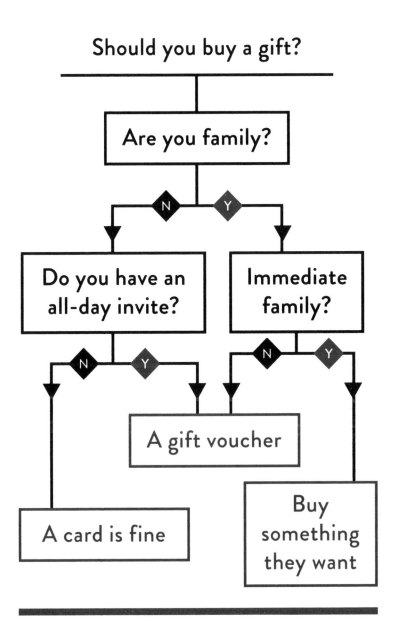

Should you buy a gift?

Are you family?

N / Y

Do you have an all-day invite?

Immediate family?

N / Y

N / Y

A gift voucher

A card is fine

Buy something they want

Stag/Hen parties

Before the wedding you may be required to attend a stag or hen party. The modern tradition is for this to be abroad for a long weekend and for it to completely ruin you for the following week.

Two days of enforced day-drinking is far from enjoyable, and actually an endurance event to get through. Stag parties are full of toxic masculinity, paintball can just fuck off. Whereas Hen parties are wall to wall cock-straws and tacky sashes.

The weekend is quickly forgotten in a haze of booze. If it is possible to skip this event, do. You can attend the inevitable smaller local event.

Leaving for a Stag do and coming back with a destroyed life

Would you give a fuck?

You're invited on a Stag/Hen party, of someone you barely know, that involves expensive flights to somewhere hot and a long weekend with arseholes. Do you...

A
Not go.

B
Go, but take a back seat and try not to spend too much.

C
Go fucking mental and get a tattoo.

A
You gave zero fucks

B
You gave some fucks

C
You gave absolute zero fucks

Christmas

Christmas can bring unnecessary stress and financial burdens.

Reduce the tat
Stop buying a load of shit for people. Nobody needs all of that
plastic shit that will end up in the ocean. Try to buy one or two
meaningful presents for people you love.

Be happy with what you have
You're not Nigella. Enjoy what you can do and don't try
to keep up with an idealised view of a perfect Christmas.

Socialise, but only if you want to
There's a lot of pressure around Christmas to attend social events. If you
don't feel up to it then don't go. Contact like-minded people who might
also be struggling with anxiety and organise a low-key, low-stress event.

**Live footage of you heading towards the chocolate tin right
after consuming your body weight in roast potatoes**

"I ONLY GO OUT TO GET ME A FRESH APPETITE FOR BEING ALONE"

Lord Byron

"OI SHELLEY, LET'S GET FUCKED UP"

Also Lord Byron after four Jagerbombs

Real world problems

Politics, budgets, finances, all of that shit.

Real world problems

These are the problems you will face when doing all your serious adulting. Finances, knowing about politics and the news. All the heavy shit.

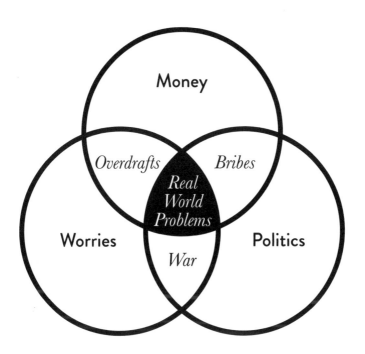

Politics

Politics rule our daily lives, everything from when bin day is to how much tax we pay. Most of us are in a bubble, particularly on social media, with our own views repeated back to us, and we think everyone thinks the same as we do. So it comes as something of a surprise when a referendum happens and you realise half the country is on the other side of the fence to you. To give zero fucks you can either decide that you can't really change anything and pretend that politics isn't happening or you can give zero fucks what people think and get politically active!

Would you give a fuck?

You're talking to someone and it becomes obvious they are stupid and have differing political views from your own. Do you...

A
Point out their wrongs but write them off as a lost cause.

B
Smile and agree with all their shit opinions.

C
Punch them square in the face.

A
You gave zero fucks

B
You gave too many fucks

C
You gave absolute zero fucks

The news

News on TV and in the paper is often bleak and full of fear. There are terrible things happening in the world all the time and watching them play out in front of you whilst you sit passively, not able to do anything about what you are seeing, can be hard.

In recent years, with 24-hour rolling news, the problem has become worse. You can now be overwhelmed by a developing news story for hours without actually learning anything new. To combat this, read or watch the news at the same time each day and allow stories to develop properly before forming opinions.

Read beyond the headline

Many headlines are written like clickbait and sensationalise the story way beyond what actually happened.

Don't get news from social media

For fuck's sake don't use Facebook to get news.

Confirmation bias

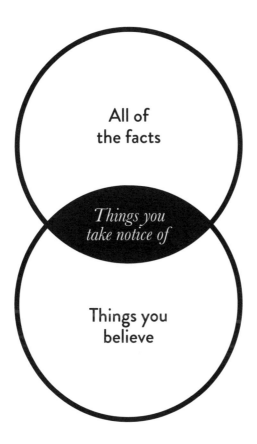

All of
the facts

*Things you
take notice of*

Things you
believe

99%

OF THINGS YOU WORRY ABOUT ABOUT NEVER HAPPEN

Money worries

Money, or lack of it, can, ironically, be your single biggest expenditure of fucks in your day-to-day life. If you can formulate a way out of debt, even if it's a five-year plan, that can help to instil some hope that there is a way out and that one day you can be debt free.

Look at your monthly budget (if you don't have one now would be a good time to work one out) and figure out where you can cut out the pointless things you're spending money on.

Make
the money

↗ ↘

Want the
things

Buy the
things

↖ ↙

Run out
of money

Repeat until dead.

Things breaking

The second law of thermodynamics on entropy states that "given enough time things will eventually get fucked up".

Fridges break, dishwashers go kaput and cars grind to a halt. It's part of the experience of owning such things, unless we are talking about a Nokia 3310. That shit is unbreakable.

So when something inevitably breaks around you, accept it as part of the natural order of things. If you're any good at fixing things then crack on and if you're not, what harm can a little tinker do before you cart it off to a skip?

Can it be fixed?

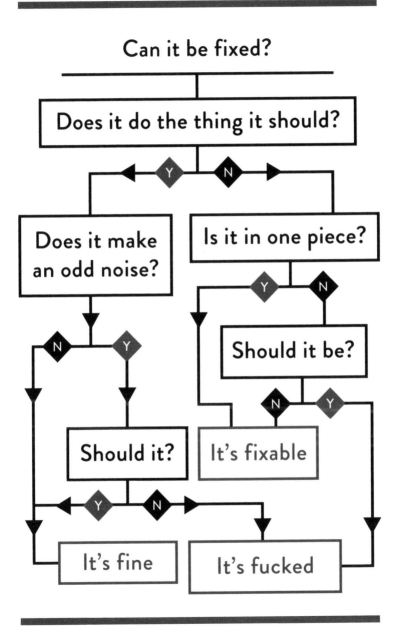

Dealing with people

Interacting with pricks, giving fucks to strangers who you will never see again.

Dealing with people

When dealing with the general public you can run into all manner of worries and stresses. The majority of people are just simply awful. All the more reason to give zero fucks when around them.

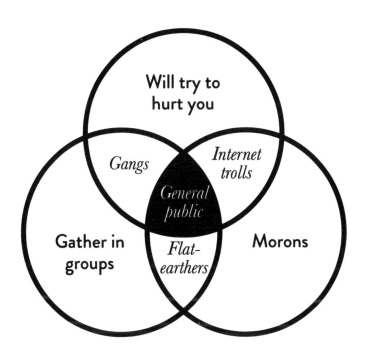

Accepting compliments

Most people love seeking recognition but when it comes they don't quite know what to do with it.

There might be a self-deprecating part of you inside that wants to downplay the compliment or even reject it completely. By doing this you might think you're showing humility but you're actually telling the person who gave you the compliment that their opinion was wrong. Accept the compliment with a simple "thank you".

The compliment	Do say	Don't say
Your top is gorgeous!	Thank you.	It was on sale and it's got a mark. Yuck.
You're so good at that!	Thank you.	You could do the same, I'm nothing special.
This tastes great!	Thank you.	It's from a jar!
You're beautiful!	Thank you.	Shut up, I'm a mess.
You're looking slim!	Thank you.	I ate a trifle this morning.

Embarrassment

People as a rule want to be accepted by society so when something happens to make you stand out you can feel crippling embarrassment.

Acknowledge what happened
Some things can't be hidden and can be made worse if you try to hide them, for example a really noisy blow-off. You should own that, it was obvious it was you. So you've spilled some wine down yourself? Style it out, pour more, pour it over your head.

Don't take yourself too seriously
People might laugh at you, but if you can laugh with them it will help your crippling cringe. Everybody makes mistakes and you're just throwing your most recent mistake on the pile.

Off to the shops to purchase some fucks as you clearly left the house without any

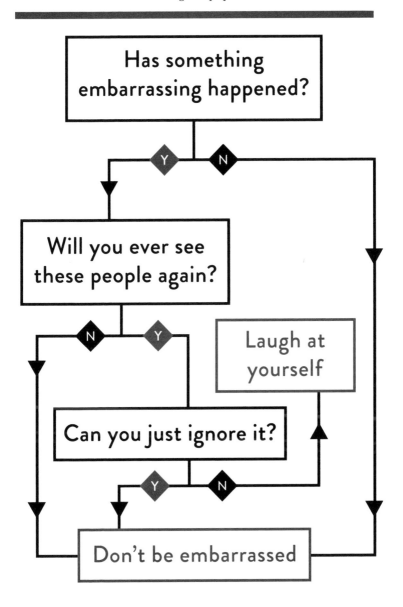

Apologies

Admitting when you're wrong isn't easy,
but it is important. Saying sorry can be hard.

It can also be far too easy to find yourself saying sorry
constantly for things that you have no control over or don't
need to apologise for. Cutting out all those unnecessary
apologies is a vital part of giving zero fucks.

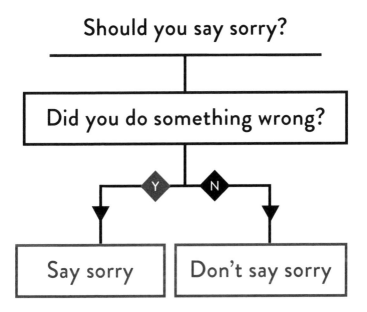

Social media

Social media is full of people you don't know that well wanting you to give a fuck about their lives. It's also a place where people like to argue about things that don't matter.

Not once has an argument on Facebook been won by anyone. Both people come away looking like fools for even trying to reason with the other.

Should you post this?

Are you being an arsehole?

Y — N

Will someone be offended?

Y — N

No.

Someone will always be offended. Post whatever you like.

Toxic people

You may have people around you who just make life harder. They might constantly put you down or undermine you or try to control your decisions. You don't have room in your life for people like this.

Get them gone
Removing a toxic person from your life can be really hard as they tend to want to hang around like a fart in a sleeping bag.

Start by creating distance from them. There is nothing wrong in avoiding people who hurt you. Don't feel the need to explain why and don't engage in an argument with them. It's not a debate.

A Venn diagram showing where toxic people should be in your life

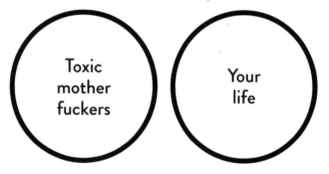

Would you give a fuck?

You've recently made a positive life choice
that a friend doesn't agree with. Do you...

A

Carry on regardless,
fuck them.

B

Send them dog
shit in the post.

C

Meet to discuss your
feelings and come to
an agreement.

A
You gave
zero fucks

B
You gave way too
many fucks

C
You gave too
many fucks

Other people's lifestyles

How other people live and their life choices, as
long as they're not affecting your life, are pretty
much none of your fucking business.

If you're offended by something someone is doing because you
don't agree with it, try to listen to their point of view and try to
understand where they are coming from. Life is rarely black and
white and you should find some common ground somewhere.

Is this your business?

Are you part of the problem?

Y   **N**

Are you part of the solution?

Y   **N**

This is not your business

This is your business

Are these genitals any of your business?

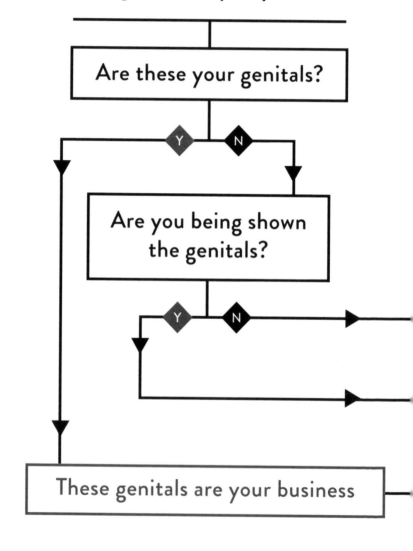

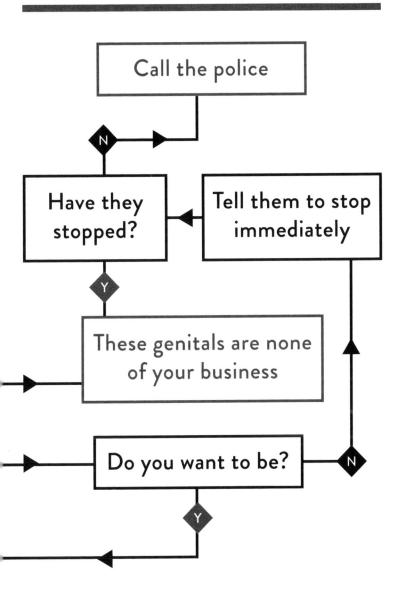

SHHH!

LET
PEOPLE
ENJOY
THINGS

Do you do things sometimes just to please people?

Good work

Stop that right now

Being too polite

It's nice to be polite, but unnecessary politeness is the scourge of those wanting to give fewer fucks.

Being less polite doesn't have to mean acting like a dick. You can be less polite but still kind (opening doors for people, saying hello to strangers, etc.). Acting in a certain way because society demands it is a ridiculous way to live.

If you're too polite to people you can rectify this by:

Letting people know when they've hurt you
If someone has hurt you, find a way to tell them. Don't be polite and carry on as if nothing happened.

Putting yourself first
Always putting yourself last isn't healthy or good for you. You can't help others if you never look after you.

Not doing favours for idiots
Being too polite leads to others taking advantage of your good nature. Don't do favours for idiots.

Standing out
It's not rude to stand out and be different from others. You're not saying that you disagree with their lifestyle, you just want to do it differently.

Not being a prick

Giving zero fucks doesn't mean you have license to swan around acting like a complete dickhead. Just because you're having fun that doesn't mean others should suffer.

There are of course bigots and prudes in the world who will be offended whatever you do. Simply work out how much you want to offend those people and crack on.

I'm considerably better than you.

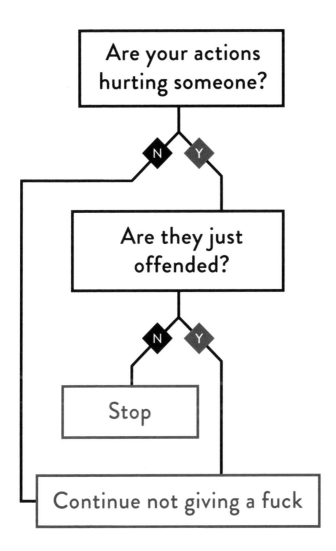

Self-care

Keeping all your best fucks stored up for you

Self-care

Being gentle with yourself. Caring for yourself should be the first place you spend fucks. If you're not cared for yourself, you can't spend any of your precious fucks anywhere.

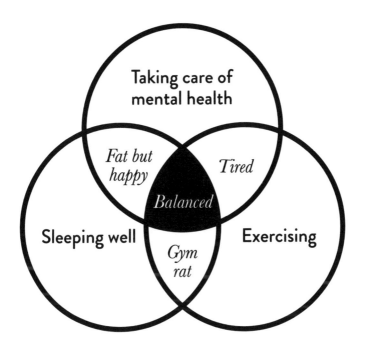

Sleeping

Sleep is where you recover from all the nonsense you went through in the day. Your brain sifts through all the twattery and files it under "bullshit". If all goes well, it wakes you up after 8 hours of studious filing. If you're not getting enough sleep there are files left all over the place and the next day is going to be a shitstorm. A regular bedtime might sound like giving too many fucks but it really is the only way to give the least amount of fucks each and every day.

The insomnia paradox

The amount of sleep you have is inversely proportional
to the anxiety you have about your lack of sleep.

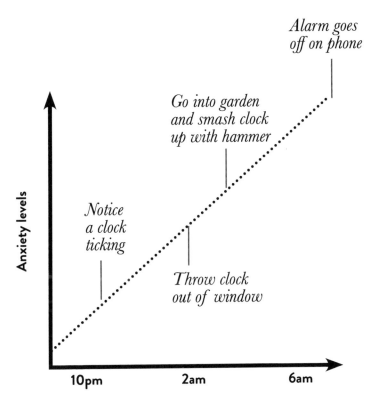

Exercise

Being physically active in the day is good not only for your body but also for your mental health.

If you're new to them, gyms can be intimidating places full of people who you might perceive to be judging you. This is a classic case of thinking everyone cares about you as much as you do. The reality is that they are either too busy staring in the mirrors at their own bodies or hoping that you notice what they are doing and are impressed with their physique.

Running to the shops in your slippers and accidentally setting a new 100m World Record

Would you give a fuck?

You go to a new gym. You're out of shape, you know no one and all the equipment is different from what you're used to. Do you...

A

Take a deep breath and ask for help.

B

Blag your way through using some equipment and take some selfies.

C

Leave immediately. Never return.

You gave zero fucks

You gave too many fucks

You gave way too many fucks

Allowing yourself to have fun

Giving too many fucks means restricting the amount of fun you can have. The only real restriction is you. Maybe you think you don't have time, or that you need to spend money, but that's not always the case.

Spontaneous fun is the best fun
Don't worry about having fun things planned, go with the flow if a situation arises for fun. Create fun opportunities.

Do little things for you
It might be giving a fake name for your coffee at Starbucks or playing a tiny practical joke on someone. Little pieces of fun that litter your day make it brighter.

Conditions won't always be perfect
There is always something more important or more serious and adult to do, but those things will still be there after the fun.

Make time
You seem to make time to stare endlessly at your phone, so you can easily afford to spend five minutes making a hat from kitchen implements.

**All dressed up and ready to leave, you
remember you're dead inside**

"NEVER APOLOGISE, NEVER EXPLAIN"

The Duke of Wellington

"DARLING, I'M SORRY, I CAN EXPLAIN!"

Also the Duke of Wellington

What you eat

Eating too many calories, or not enough? That's your business. If you want to eat healthily or devote more time to the carb food group you go right ahead.

If you have no idea what you are eating or are worried you are eating too much, keep a food journal. Then you can work from the actual facts of what you are eating to see if you want to change something.

Looking everywhere for whoever the fuck asked you

Should you eat the whole pizza?

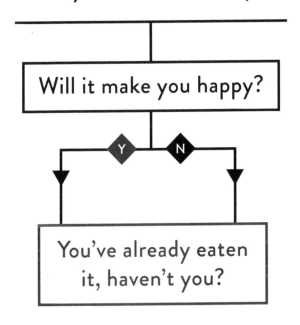

Clothes

Clothes can be fashionable, functional or fun. They can be expressions of who we are. People judge us on what we wear. Hence most people don't like to stand out or look silly.

Fashions change fast. If you're adhering to a trend or trying to remain on top you're going to end up spending too much money and looking silly, or being outdated. So find something you like wearing and do your own thing. As long as genitals are covered you're within the law and you can wear whatever you like. *How to Give Zero Fucks* does not cover advice on defending yourself against a charge of indecent exposure.

It's called fashion, sweetie, maybe try it sometime?

Would you give a fuck?

You want to wear dungarees. Do you...

A

Try them on, feel silly,
not buy them.

B

Wear the shit out of
some dungarees.

C

Think they won't suit
you so not even try.

You gave too
many fucks

You gave
zero fucks

You gave way too
many fucks

"I DON'T DO FASHION, I AM FASHION"

Coco Chanel

"*SNIFFS* THESE ARE GOOD FOR ANOTHER DAY"

You, you disgusting animal

Regrets

Regrets are about things that happened in the past that bring you sorrow or shame, but they are just that, in the past.

Dealing with your regrets with zero fucks is a three-stage process:

1. Accept what happened
You can't change it, it was a fuck up.
Don't brush the feelings aside but also don't wallow in them.

2. Learn
Make better choices in future. Learn from
what happened and move on. Try not to fuck up again.

3. Time
Given enough time most regrets will make a good story in the pub.
So you shit yourself, yes, but telling people about it years later will
give you the final victory.

Tragedy + Time = Comedy

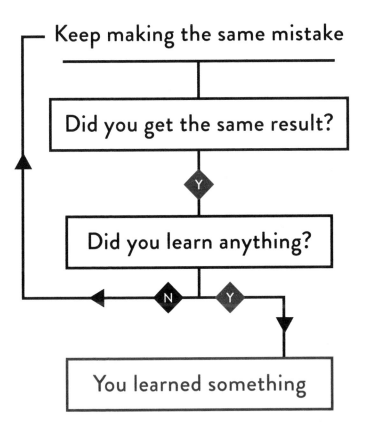

Getting old

As you get older you begin to feel like you're falling apart. Knees stop working and backs become fucked. Apart from the standard existential crisis that this raises, the physical side effects of ageing can be a bit of a kick in the nuts/tits.

Think of your body like an old car: it needs care and attention but it also needs a long run every now and then to keep the battery charged. Use your body as and when you can before it gets carted off on the back of a lorry to be crushed. (They don't crush bodies, just cars... this analogy has broken down.)

Would you give a fuck?

You notice a new wrinkle on your forehead. Do you...

A

Show people all day and remind them that we all die.

B

Buy an expensive anti-wrinkle cream, with Bollox®.

C

Draw little eyes above it and call it Gerald.

You gave too many fucks

You gave way too many fucks

You gave zero fucks

Being bitter

If you have resentments, unsolved altercations
and bitterness you need to let that shit go.

Bitterness is a poison that eats you up and makes you act in ways you
never thought you would see yourself behaving. Your bitterness and
hate aren't affecting the person who caused them but simply making
you feel sorry for yourself, angry or hateful.

Bitterness fades with time and perspective but left unchecked it can be
the gremlin in your system that constantly fucks things up.

**Keeping the little book of resentments
up to date in case you forget someone**

Acknowledge

Write down on a piece of paper who hurt you
and why you can't let it go. Acknowledge
why and how you are being bitter.

Let it go

Walk away from it. Easier said than
done, but vital.

Forgive

Whoever you're forgiving might be a complete
shit but once you forgive them you can begin to
move on with your sassy new life. Now breathe.

Learning to fail

You're human, you make mistakes. It's what you do best.
Learning not just to fail, but to enjoy failure, is a valuable trait
of someone who gives zero fucks.

Without failure you will never know how far you can go.
Your true capabilities will remain untapped. This could be for
dull stuff like work but it could also be that you don't know
how many marshmallows you can fit in your mouth before
you are sick on your shoes.

When you fail you learn to come back stronger, with new tactics
and ideas that help you. Perhaps fold the marshmallows before
putting them in? Maybe try a drink of water first?

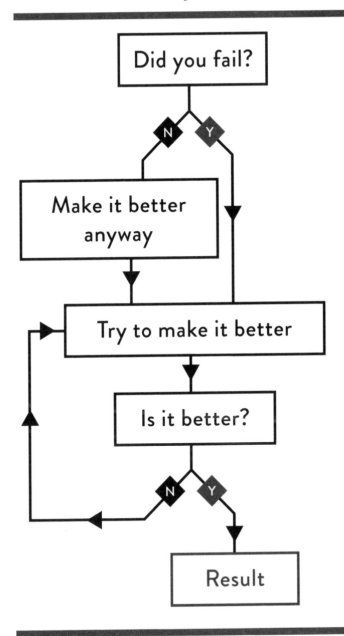

"TRY AGAIN, FAIL AGAIN, FAIL BETTER"

Samuel Beckett

"FOR FUCK'S SAKE, ONE MORE TRY"

Samuel Beckett later that day

Coping with anxiety

If you find yourself having to ask "Is there something I should be worried about?" then you are probably suffering from anxiety. It's a feeling of fear of things that are about to happen (although many of them never will). It's hard to not give a fuck about a fear you are having that feels very real.

Think through what is real. What are truths that you know? If it's too much to deal with, take yourself physically out of the situation, take a breath and notice your surroundings. Mindfulness and meditation can also help you focus on these things.

Opening the door to another day of this shit

Would you give a fuck?

You have an exam coming up. Do you...

A

Revise. Revise. Revise. Revise. Revise. Revise.

B

Do your best. You can always retake.

C

Not turn up.

You gave too many fucks

You gave zero fucks

You gave absolute zero fucks

What people think anxiety feels like

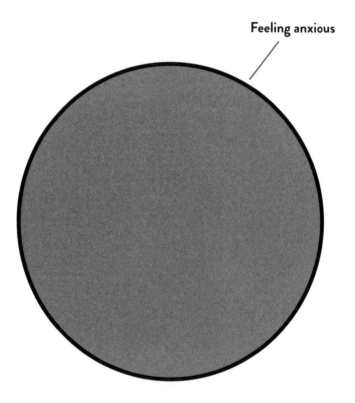

Feeling anxious

What anxiety feels like

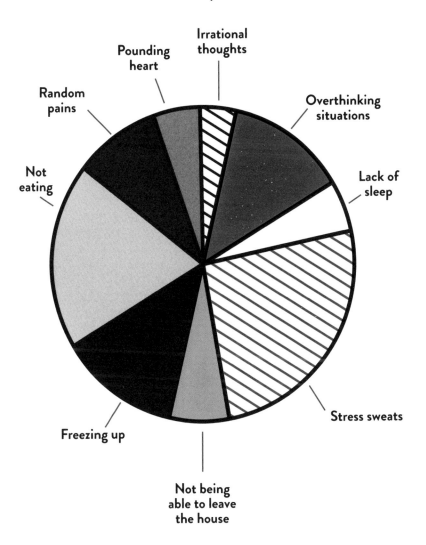

Some "me time"

Having "me time" is a way to signal to those around you that you are spending some fucks on taking care of yourself for a while.

Block out all the everyday distractions and spend some time with something you find enjoyable.

If loved ones struggle with you wanting time away from them, offer a reminder that far from being selfish, "me time" will be mentally and physically refreshing and you will be able to return and give a fuck about their bullshit once more.

You can choose whatever makes you happy to be your "me time". It might be a deep bath or meditation or just staring at a fucking wall.

**Having your "me time" with a copy of *Grazia*
knowing full well that the kids are kicking off next door**

Recipe for a "basic bitch" bath

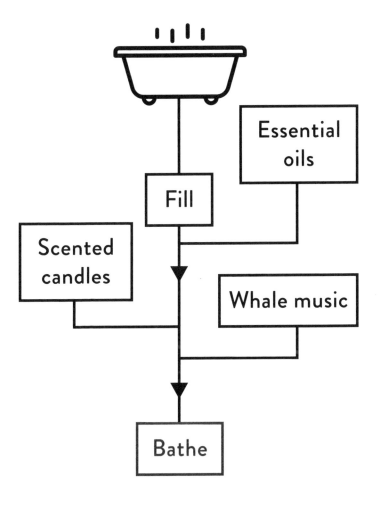

I can't be fucked to write this any more.

About the author

Stephen Wildish is the author of *How to Vegan*, *How to Swear* and *How to Adult*. He's also a vegan who's teetotal and into Crossfit. He doesn't know what to tell you about first!

Stephen is the current 100m and 200m sack-race world-record holder.

He couldn't have been fucked to write this shit without the help of Jake Allnutt, Michelle Warner and Sam Frencho.

1 3 5 7 9 10 8 6 4 2

Pop Press, an imprint of Ebury Publishing
20 Vauxhall Bridge Road
London SW1V 2SA

Pop Press is part of the Penguin Random House group of companies whose
addresses can be found at global.penguinrandomhouse.com

First published by Pop Press in 2020

www.penguin.co.uk

A CIP catalogue record for this book is available from the British Library

ISBN 9781529107579

Printed and bound by TBB, a.s. Slovakia

Penguin Random House is committed to a
sustainable future for our business, our readers
and our planet. This book is made from Forest
Stewardship Council® certified paper.